The Great Lakes
Atlantic Ocean
Gulf of Mexico

SRAonline.com

Mc Graw Hill SRA

Printed in the U.S.A.

Send all inquiries to:
SRA/McGraw-Hill
4400 Easton Commons
Columbus, OH 43219

ISBN: 978-0-07-612512-8
MHID: 0-07-612512-2

9 10 11 12 LHN 24 23 22

Hurry and the Monarch

BY ANTOINE Ó FLATHARTA
ILLUSTRATED BY MEILO SO

For Aisling—A.Ó.F. For my father—M.S.

Hurry the Texas tortoise is starting to think about winter when out of the bright October sky a monarch butterfly lands on his back.

"What do you call this place?"
asks the monarch.

"Wichita Falls," says Hurry. "And that's my back you're standing on."

"Wichita Falls. Not far enough," says the monarch.

"Not far enough for what?" asks Hurry.

"For staying," replies the monarch.

With that, the monarch opens her wings and flies off Hurry's back. Eye level with Hurry now, the monarch seems fascinated with the old tortoise.

"How long have you been here?" asks the monarch.

"Seems like forever," says Hurry.

"Maybe one day you'll break out of that shell, grow wings, and fly away," says the monarch.

"I doubt it," says Hurry.

"It happened to me," replies the monarch, thinking about that extraordinary morning when she first opened her wings.

“Where did this happen?” asks Hurry.
“Far away, in a place called Canada.
In a garden just like this.”
“Why did you leave?” asks Hurry.
“The days got colder,” says the monarch. “What do *you* do when the days get colder?”
“Sleep,” answers Hurry. “Cold days always change back into warm days if you wait. “

"I don't have time for that," says the monarch, flying away from the garden.

She joins more monarchs. They turn the sky orange as
they continue their journey south toward Sweetwater.

Back in the garden, a cloud passes over the sun and Hurry shuts his eyes. As the old tortoise begins to dream …

the monarch travels on, resting at night in places you would expect to see a butterfly rest.

And sometimes in places you would not.

Each new day brings new sights.

Sometimes a day brings danger.

But the monarch survives, flying now toward Eagle Pass, then over the waters of the Rio Grande into Mexico.

On and on she flies until finally, one November evening, she finds it. The warm green forest she has been searching for. She hangs from a bough, adding her tired wings to the soft murmur of a million others.

The monarch in flight from winter knows
she has found the perfect place.

Spring returns to Hurry's garden. He slowly opens his eyes and feels the warmth of the sun. "Never fails," thinks Hurry.

Then one morning, the monarch also returns. "So where are you going now?" asks Hurry. "Back to the beginning," answers the monarch. "Do you mean Canada?" asks Hurry. "Possibly," says the monarch.

"Butterflies can be infuriatingly mysterious," thinks Hurry, watching the monarch lay eggs on a milkweed plant. Then she flies away.

In the town of Stillwater, she flies in through an open window and things it might be nice to rest her worn wings for a while in the folds of a sun-colored curtain. For a while becomes forever.

Back in the garden, over
by the milkweed plant,
Hurry sees a newborn
caterpillar.
"Hello," says Hurry, but
the caterpillar doesn't
answer.

He is too busy eating the
milkweed leaves.

Hurry watches and waits as the caterpillar grow, shedding skin after skin, then crawling away to hide under a twig.

But this garden is Hurry's whole world and there is little in it that is hidden from him.

In the weeks that follow, Hurry sees an amazing transformation happen right in front of his still and patient eyes. A new monarch emerges from the shell, wet and wrinkled.

For a while, he clings
to his empty shell,
waiting for his wings
to expand and dry in
the warm sunshine.

After a few hours, the monarch spreads his strong new wings and flies toward Hurry, landing on his back. "What do you call this place?" asks the monarch. "Here we go again," says Hurry as the monarch opens his wings and flies off Hurry's back.

"What's your hurry?" asks Hurry.
"I'm off to see the world. What do
you think it's like?" asks the butterfly.
"I imagine—" says Hurry slowly,
"I imagine that it's like my garden.
A place full of astonishing things."
"I can't wait," says the young
monarch, flying away.

Afterword

The migration of the monarch butterfly is one of the most amazing journeys in the insect world. Like all butterflies, the monarch begins life as a tiny egg, which a female monarch lays on the underside of the leaf of a milkweed plant. Three to six days later, a caterpillar is born. At first the caterpillar is so small it can barely be seen. It rows very fast, gorging itself on milkweed leaves. In about nine to fourteen days, it is fully grown. It then crawls away from the milkweed plant to find a safe place to pupate. This is the stage where it forms a chrysalis, or shell. In about two weeks, it is possible to make out the shape of the a butterfly through the transparent chrysalis. Then the chrysalis cracks open and the butterfly comes out.

Monarchs born in early autumn are the ones that make the extraordinary journey to Mexico. Shorter, colder days in places like Canada send the monarchs south across the United States of America, traveling distances of 50 to 80 and sometimes even 125 miles per day. Finally, after traveling almost 2,000 miles, they arrive in the fir forests of Mexico in early November. They blanket the forests with millions of flashing wings as they hang from tree boughs. One tree bough alone can contain as many as 20,000 butterflies. A whole colony can contain up to 6 million monarchs per acre. The sight and sound of millions of monarchs together is one of the wonders of the world.

They stay until March, when they begin their long journey north. The monarch that left Canada will never get back home, but its great-great-great-grandchild will. There, the following autumn, the journey will begin again. On the journey back to Canada, newborn monarchs often rest at some of the exact spots where monarchs flying to Mexico rested months ago.

The monarch butterfly protects itself by the bright orange marking on its wings, which tells birds and other predators that it might be poisonous. But other dangers face the monarch. Its winter resting grounds keep getting smaller as the fir forests are destroyed for wood and for housing developments.

The monarchs that make the journey to Mexico normally can live up to eight months or more; the spring and summer generations live the usual butterfly life span—between four and six weeks. This is very different from the life span of the other character in this story, the land tortoise. A slow-moving reptile that carries its home on its back, the tortoise is a very old life-form, older even than the dinosaur. It can live up to 100 years or more—a total contrast to the short, busy life of the monarch butterfly.

CANADA
U.S.A.
Wich ta Falls
Texas
Pacific Ocean
MEXICO